THE JOY OF HEAVEN 7

The Day of The Lord Comes To Earth

Daniel Leske

."...they shall MOUNT up with wings as eagles..." Isaiah 40:31

The Joy of Heaven 7: The Day of the Lord Comes To Earth by Daniel Leske
Copyright © 2020 by Daniel Leske
All Rights Reserved.
ISBN: 978-1-59755-575-3

Published by: ADVANTAGE BOOKS™
                 Longwood, Florida, USA
                 www.advbookstore.com

Library of Congress Catalog Number: 2019957984

First Printing: January 2020
20 21 22 23 24 25 26   10 9 8 7 6 5 4 3 2 1
Printed in the United States of America

Prelude

There may be a season of time on earth before "The Joy of Heaven 7" takes place, yet by book 5, the decision could come at any time if the Lord decides to shorten the days.

Life on earth will parallel with the words of Revelation and other books of the Bible that talk about life on earth before book 7, but life on earth will fall prey to the powers of the enemy as this season and warfare increases!

The spiritual warfare increases between God and Lucifer, with mankind caught in the middle, seeing, feeling, and reacting in ways that are not always pleasing to God.

Now read book 7 with that in mind as the earth has placed itself into the final battle between good and evil.

DANIEL

Daniel Leske

List of Characters

Wee Angel:	She has white hair and is always a little smaller than any other angels.
Felicia:	She is about 8 or 9 years old in stature with blonde hair.
Angel Gabriella:	Angel Daniella and Angel Gabriella are identical twin angels.
Angel Daniella:	Angel Daniella and Angel Gabriella are identical twin angels.
Sir William	(Revelation) A very SPECIAL white winged horse.
David, Joshua	Leaders of heaven's army
Jesus:	In front and leading the Lord's army.
Lord God Almighty:	Rules heaven and earth from the throne.
All the little angels:	After it is over they seek and greet Wee Angel, Felicia, Angel Daniella and Angel Gabriella.

Others from Bible leading units, with the archangels, powerful angels and the powerful white winged horses with riders. The thousands and thousands of angels in praise as Jesus and army leave heaven's lands.

In book 7 there is a time, maybe days, maybe some years before the action of this book goes into action, which is only known by Jesus, with Lord God Almighty when the Father says, "Now is the time!" With this Jesus, the archangels, angels, winged horses with riders come to earth carrying out the mission, the warfare against dragon(Lucifer) and his army. The book unveils the battle plan. At the end of the day Jesus arrives at the Mount of Olives! I suggest everyone read Revelation(use KJV only) for understanding to the trouble we are in, to why this day finally comes as explained in Old and New Testament.

Daniel Leske

Chapter 1

Outside God's City

Wee Angel and Felicia stood quietly outside of God's Holy City along the golden way by some tall pine trees. A stream quietly flowed from God's Holy City. Many birds were present singing with all their might. They saw glories high above them.

There was a special quietness in their hearts. There was a special thankfulness too! They smiled and flew upwards around some tall trees. They made many circles in heaven's skies. They felt so much love, peace and joy! Their hearts were full.

Wee Angel said to Felicia, "Let's go back to where I first saw you in heaven."

"That sounds beautiful!" smiled Felicia.

With that, both flew up into heaven's skies as Wee Angel led the way in flight.

They flew quite some time over meadows, flower areas of heaven, then finally to a vast field of lilies.

Soon they stood on the golden path where Wee Angel had met Felicia coming to heaven.

"Oh my! Oh My!" said Felicia.

Both stood and thanked the Lord, looked at the lilies, the heavenly skies, and glories from God's Holy City. It wasn't too long heavenly time that both saw a couple of very, powerful angels fly towards them. The light around them was immense, even for their heavenly eyes. Soon they knew it was Archangel Michael and Archangel Gabriel.

Now, as mentioned before, the archangels were capable of as much power as needed by God. As they flew and came nearer, they had a lot of power about them. They told Wee Angel and Felicia to follow them.

In heaven's time, they were at a vast area of grass along a stream close by huge waterfalls with glories streaming along the sides, with high pinnacles to the outside of the enormous waterfalls.

Then away in the distance, they saw the high glories from God's Holy Mountain as part of the city that was a distance away from the falls that slowly came along the mountain's edges from God's Holy Mountain.

There were many fruit trees by the base of the falls along the wide river, hedges, fields of flowers too! High above beautiful doves flew with some geese.

Soon they rested by a few apple trees, then decided to have a couple of apples while they waited there.

It wasn't too long that they saw in flight two special angels flying towards them.

They immediately knew it was Angel Gabriella and Angel Daniella. Archangel Gabriel and Archangel Michael had already left, so it was just the four that stood, talked, prayed, and thanked the Lord.

Angel Daniella said, "Angel Micah told us to fly here and wait with you.

Something is about to happen! He said to wait here."

They continued to enjoy the heavenly moments as they watched and looked at the beautiful pinnacles by the sides of the wide waterfalls. Golden paths went along the river with special courtyards for saints to visit, pray, and enjoy God's Holy City. Beautiful hedges of flowers, small stepped waterfalls, streams were present too!

Special flowered areas in and around the fruit trees, with a vast circular area where many horses could be at one time. In the distance along and away from the city were smaller mountains, and hills, plush with heavenly trees such as pines, some tall redwoods in beautiful groupings.

The tall redwoods were so awesome with hills to their sides and then higher mountains to the Holy City side, and again more pinnacles.

Daniel Leske

Chapter 2

An Important Meeting

They walked and praised the Lord for their hearts were heavy with thought, yet full of joy. They knew something significant was about to happen as the Lord wanted them to be a part of it. In heaven's time, several more winged horses flew closer to them.

They knew that these were the power riders. There were about 12 winged horses and riders. As they flew closer, they saw that Sir William was with them.

The leader of the winged horses was in front with Sir William right next to him.

Soon they landed on the grassy area, with the leader directing everyone into a row and he nodded to them but waited with the other horse and riders. In heaven's time, they saw about 20 saints come closer up a golden path along the river from on the archways into God's Holy City.

They strolled past some of the small courtyards along the golden path. In front, as they walked, they soon saw it was Jesus. Walking right beside Jesus was Paul as they continued to get closer to them.

High above and along the sides, angels were gathering slowly and hovering in heaven's skies. There was a quietness to the angels and calmness to the scene. Jesus and the others walked towards the leader of the winged horses.

Paul nodded towards Wee Angel and Felicia, then said to them that they should wait where they were for a while yet!

Soon two more riders on white-winged horses landed there. It was David and Joshua. They, with Jesus, leader of riders, Paul, and the other saints, walked to the courtyard of apple trees right along a beautiful river.

They continued to talk, as more angels flew and hovered in the heavenly skies above everyone.

Daniel Leske

Wee Angel said, "This is something very important!"

With this, Joshua came towards them and said they would be coming with them. He said that the saints that were with Jesus and Paul were elders of heaven that helped with the decisions that Jesus talked for their advice and wisdom.

With that, Joshua turned and went back to the meeting with the others.

In a short time, about 15 more angels flew and landed close by Wee Angel, Felicia, Angel Daniella, and Angel Gabriella. One of them walked and said that they would be flying close by them when the meeting was finished! Then they walked more towards the winged horses and riders that were all lined up in perfect rows.

The scene was an awesome scene of a powerful meeting in heaven. Angels still were flying into the area high above and around the area in a huge circle.

Heaven at this time seemed very quiet and still in a way that even Wee Angel was not used to feeling it this way! They looked at each other, sensing something mighty, but didn't know what!

They prayed and were still as they waited for Jesus and the others to finish their meeting.

Chapter 3

Now is the Time

In heavenly time, the meeting continued with angels above, doves in flight nearby, with the glories of God's Holy City. Soon Wee Angel looked and saw all the elders kneeling in prayer.

She said, "They are starting to have prayer time. Let's all kneel too."

The riders by their horses now were kneeling. Paul, David, Joshua, the archangels, with all the elders knelt as Jesus stood and lifted his arms saying, "Father, we now trust in you as we go and carry out this mission as we have talked and I have made the decision that NOW IS THE TIME!"

As they stood, a large arm of Lord God Almighty flashed through the heavenly sky above and the voice of Jesus, and the voice of the Lord God by the power of the Holy Spirit. They spoke loudly together as one to all the angels and everyone present, "OUR WILL BE DONE!"

With this, Paul, the leaders of the riders, David, Joshua and elders all gave heavenly hugs, including Jesus.

Jesus said to David, Joshua, and the leader, "Let's get it done!"

Paul slowly turned to the elders and nodded. They then slowly walked aside, stood and watched David, Joshua, the riders mount their white-winged horses. Paul was to stay at the Holy City with the elders because of his responsibilities for Jesus.

Wee Angel said to Felicia as Angel Daniella and Angel Gabriella watched, "Remember the Bible states, "They shall mount and rise with wings as eagles."

They continued to mount these beautiful horses. Jesus slowly walked to Revelation as he got down on his knees in humility. Jesus walked, then mounted Revelation to carry out his will, the will of the Holy Spirit, the will of the Father, the will of Joshua, David, Paul, and the elders.

Soon they were mounted and stood ready for flight. The fifteen angels were very close to Wee Angel, Felicia, Angel Daniella, and Angel Gabriella. Four of the riders came with their winged horses.

Angel Guardian of the fifteen angels said, "Each of you will ride behind one of these riders as Joshua and David will be leading formations because they have much to do, so you will be riding with these riders. We will be flying right next to your horses and around your horses for your protection."

Soon they were seated on white horses behind the riders.

Chapter 4

Onward

Paul and the elders stood and watched as Jesus and the riders sat on these beautiful white-winged horses as they opened their mighty wings like eagles.

Soon they were in flight! They circled the area as Paul and the elders continued to watch them.

There was a stillness to heaven like never before!

This stillness was so intense in everyone's hearts, including the riders, angels and our little ones.

All creation seemed to sense the will of God and just knew his mighty power, as Jesus was in front of the riders on Revelation.

He winged slowly onward just above the trees and river, flowers, golden paths. The other angels flew alongside them and to the front of them. Then in time, another huge formation of winged horses flew closer to them — one from the left and one from the right. Solomon led one of the formations and Simon Peter led the other formation of winged horses with riders.

Obadiah with Felicia, Matthew with Wee Angel, James with Angel Gabriella, Bartholomew with Angel Daniella.

Then these formations slowly flew in behind the others as Jesus led the white-winged horses on Revelation. Angels were gathering to the sides way ahead of the formation and hovered ready to sing glories and praises,

They flew just above heaven's lands as more and more angels quickly flew from all directions.

Soon Wee Angel said, "My! All the angels again to the sides!"

Way ahead of them to the left and the right were many glories of beautiful lights that streamed upwards from heaven's lands. In the glories were thousands and thousands of angels. The riders on white-winged horses continued to fly straight ahead above heaven's lands through the valley of glories filled with angels hovering and praising the Lord.

The valley was now deep ahead of them as far as they could see! Soon from the left came another formation of horses with hundreds of riders being led by Abraham. From the right came Moses and his formation of winged horses. They again flew in place behind the massive formation of white-winged horses.

The valley of angels was now wider and higher, as high as they could see upwards! Glories were everywhere.

"Glory to the Father!" the angels said, "Glory to the Father!"

The sides far and away from them went upward as they formed a vast valley of angels with glories as far as their eyes could see ahead and continued forming ahead as they flew along above the lands.

"Glory to Jesus!"

"Glory to the Father!"

"Glory!"

"Praise to the Father!"

"Praise the Lord!"

"Praise Jesus!"

Now the angels were shouting in unison!

"Jesus!" "Jesus!" "Jesus!" "Jesus!"

Jesus, who was sitting on Revelation, flew slowly onward! The trumpets by angels would blow a mighty sound as it seemed to travel all the way across heaven. Then more shouts!

"Jesus!" "Jesus!" "Jesus!" "Jesus!"

"Jesus!" "Jesus!" "Jesus!" "Jesus!"

Onward they flew!

Then in a vast opening between the glories of angels to the sides, two more huge formations of winged horses and riders each slowly flew closer to the enormous formation of winged horses and riders.

Matthew said to Felicia, "Zechariah is leading the formation from the left. Jeremiah is leading the formation of winged horses on the right."

Onward they flew with these horses, taking their place behind the others. Still, way to the front was the wide valley with angels high into the heavenly skies. Yet these riders on their white-winged horses were still in slow flight just above the lands of heaven.

Daniel Leske

Chapter 5

The Mission to Earth

"Praise the Father!"

"Glory to Jesus!"

"Mighty One!"

"Holy of Holies!"

"Jesus!"

"Hallelujah!"

"Hallelujah!"

"Hallelujah!"

"Jesus!"

The voices of the angels rang with shouts of glory. Then more horns would sound. They continued to shout and praise the Lord. The massive formation with Jesus on Revelation flew slowly across more of heaven's lands.

Then from the left through another wide opening in the valley, another formation with hundreds of winged horses and riders.

Obadiah said to "Felicia, this formation has Samuel as its leader. The formation on the right has Aaron as its leader."

They flew in and behind the massive formation of hundred's and hundred's of white-winged horses, still across heaven's lands through the valley of angels praising the Lord. The shouting continued as Wee Angel said to Matthew to look at the horizon as a valley of clouds was going upwards away from heaven's lands.

The valley formed by clouds was still way in the distance, but Jesus led the formation closer to where they would be flying upwards away from heaven's lands. Along the valley sides angels hovered with the sounds of glory as they continued:

"Jesus!"

"Jesus!"

"Jesus!"

"Praise to the Father!"

"Hallelujah to the King!"

Onward they flew!

Soon all the winged horses and riders slowly flew upwards between the clouds with thousands and thousands of angels to their sides, upward away from heaven's lands. Upward on a mission that has been talked about over and over by so many on earth over the hundreds of years.

Jesus and the power riders were now in flight in a valley formed by clouds. They flew away from heaven's lands on the mission to save and repossess earth and those that would be alright by the time all of this was finished there.

Obadiah said to Felicia, "All of the leaders of the formations of the horses have already been informed to what they must do there. Jesus had said when the time comes, the power riders have been briefed and informed about the plan."

Onward the white-winged horses flew more and more away from heaven's land in the broad valley of clouds. The horses now flew faster and faster, as angels were still present along the sides with the clouds behind them.

Chapter 6

A Thief in the Night

Jesus was in front, riding on Revelation. All the riders on their white-winged horses followed behind him. All in an orderly manner in rows, yet evenly away from each other. There were thousands and thousands of winged horses with riders.

The riders had on the most highly protective attire. They were dressed much the same as before, but their attire was such that high powered light forces that could come against them would not penetrate their attire.

Their garments were off white made of an extremely fine mesh so that no force of light energy could penetrate or hurt as we know it. So at a distance, they indeed looked like a fine linen clothing in appearance to the earthly eyes.

Again gems on the shoulders with a bluish trim to their outfits with dark golden boots. The gems had the colors of green, golden, red's and blues. The horses also had a fine mesh covering over their backs and around the mane.

The riders had flaming swords by their sides. They were with gold and silver handles in a sheath of different shades of gold and silver. The swords in the sheaths had a round crossbar and fires came from the bar. It also was cup-like with the soft fires and flames that could quickly become an intense ray of firelight against any enemy in battle. These same swords could also send light to ensnare demons and serpents of Lucifer to hold them still and ready till known their destiny.

The sheaths had beautiful gems of reds, blues, lavenders, purples, greens, as they flashed beautiful colors of light!

The power of light was so strong about them that an earthly eye would only see the light and some of the image of the horse and rider.

Onward they flew!

They flew more and more away from heaven's lands.

Wee Angel, Felicia, Angel Gabriella, and Angel Daniella had been told that the mission was to earth and that this time the mission would be carried out as everything was done and in order for Jesus to return there.

They knew this and also they knew that they were safe with the angels that flew close by them. Little was said by any of them.

Wee Angel looked at Felicia. She looked at Angel Gabriella and Angel Daniella. They had a quietness on their faces and a heaviness in their little heavenly hearts. The Lord had made sure that none of them felt any fears, only comfort and love by being with him and the riders.

There were clouds all around them as they flew through the heavens towards the earth.

As they flew more powerful angels of God's came and flew up behind the winged horses and riders. These angels were not as mighty as the archangels, but more powerful than most angels in heaven. They were now on a mission and would do the duties as Jesus and their leader had told them. There were thousands of these mighty angels all in flight right behind the horses and riders. The power of light about them was awesome. There was golden light rays that came and went away from their very being.

They were so majestic in God's beautiful creation, yet they had duties to carry out on earth, and they were eager and ready for this was their moment. They had waited a long time for this. Again Wee Angel looked at Felicia and smiled a little, holding tight to Matthew.

They continued to fly onward!

They had flown away from the angels that were shouting and praising the Lord. There were just clouds around them as they flew along following the course that headed towards earth. Tremendous fires of light glowed and burned high above with enormous bursts showing the power of the fire. It seemed like it could explode at any time with a command by Jesus.

This mighty army of God's flew quietly along in between all the clouds that formed a pathway to earth. There was a stillness in and around everyone. Yet, there was a sense of the mighty power of God, as Jesus rode on Revelation, with His vast army of riders and mighty angels that flew onwards towards the earth. It was time to bring the will of God and the laws of the earth back to the order of His Word, as had been prophesied.

Jesus was quiet and very much in command as they flew onward toward earth.

They flew onward!

Now it was a time and season of battle. A battle that had to be so that that order could be restored on the earth.

They flew onward!

Wee Angel again looked at Felicia, Angel Daniella, and Angel Gabriella. She had so much on her little heart too! So did all the angels that flew in the formation. They knew their duties as the Lord had prepared them for this time.

Within heaven's time, the clouds started to lessen a little and in the distance way ahead of them was Earth.

Daniel Leske

Chapter 7

Jericho

In the seasons before the decision made about earth, there was already a lot of turmoil. Lucifer was on a mission to slowly evolve or turn mankind into creatures like himself instead of men, women, boys and girls as God so created!

Science, medicine, electronics etc. were forcing more and more life away from the laws of God. Destruction was coming by ways devised by Lucifer and carried out in slow fashion, but leading mankind to destruction and imprisonment of the mind and soul.

Slowly an extremely terrible and powerful false system was forming over earth. Archangels were stirring winds on the earth as God's wrath was already being carried out towards earth.

Many on earth were wondering when would the Lord come to help them and peace be throughout the earth.

They flew closer and closer to earth. It was still in the distance as the riders made ready for a signal from Jesus. As far as the eyes could see were winged horses and riders, followed by thousands of angels in flight and in formation.

The thousands of angels that followed were ready and waited for their signal from the Lord.

Matthew said that they would stay in an area not too far from Jesus and Revelation, because these angels must protect Jesus and his area too!

Onward in order flew the horses, angels with mighty power of light, which glowed and surrounded them, almost like a star that was getting closer to earth, yet it was the glow of Jesus and the army behind him. Many on earth may have wonderment over this!

The earth was still at a distance but the horizons of earth started to form as they flew closer to it.

There still were clouds to their sides and still below them, yet as they flew, ahead of them they could see how the Creator formed these clouds by fire and waters.

They flew onward, with clouds to the sides and below them.

A beautiful sight to see as this heavenly army flew with earth's horizons becoming a part of their flight.

Matthew said to Wee Angel, "We are getting close to where Jesus will signal and the leaders will signal the other leaders. Be prepared for the time is soon here!"

Obadiah talked to Felicia too! He said, "Felicia, this battle will be a lot like one from the Bible. The mission is simply called by Jesus, 'Jericho!' This is how our army of angels, and riders will approach earth. 'Jericho' The whole earth is Jericho and that is our plan. It will be unfolding soon as Jesus signals us!"

Chapter 8

The Battle Begins

The horizons of earth drew closer and the clouds were lessening! Fires of God filled the skies. Then Jesus raised his right arm and motioned and pointed to his right. With this motion, a great flash of light went out and away from him, almost like lightning. It was like the right arm of God pointed with Jesus to the right as a loud crack of noise filled the sky.

Moses and Abraham started to fly their formations to the right. Then Jesus did the same with his left arm, and again a great light flashed with the crack of thunder.

The angels that followed these formations separated to follow the formations. Many winged horses stayed with Jesus, David, Joshua and some of the other leaders

Wee Angel said to Matthew, "What a beautiful sight to see them fly towards the horizons of earth, all in an orderly manner."

Matthew added, "Yes, it is, but the beauty of this will soon be gone as the battle begins!"

"Yes, I know!" quietly spoke Wee Angel.

"Just know all of you are very safe as these angels will guard and protect Jesus and us!"

The formations of horses and angels were all in flight to different places around the earth. The angels were separating as needed and going with the winged horse units to these areas.

"In time," Matthew continued, "They will be in different places all around the earth."

"My!" said Wee Angel.

In time, Jesus, with formations of white-winged horses and angels, were at the waters of the Mediterranean Sea.

It was early morning after the midnight hour!

They flew very slowly as they made ready for their appearance on earth. Many were already aware of a presence and the magnitude of this, but could not do anything, because the archangels of God were interfering with all the signals on the earth. So the earth was already seeing and feeling problems being caused by the archangels as they made the ways clear for Jesus.

He flew Revelation as they still were high in the skies on earth, and flew more towards land as so spoken about by the Word. The formations followed Jesus as they flew towards his land, the land of Israel, which is the land He said that He would protect from all the nations of the earth that would rise up against his people.

He flew Revelation close to its shores, then with a loud voice, out of his mouth came a sharp two edged sword of tremendous light that soared quickly across the skies in flight as a shout by Jesus.

He said, "Behold, I come!"

It was like the thunder of this light ripping through all the skies going entirely around the earth as if everyone could hear and see this tremendous sword of light and voice of God speak, "Behold I come!"

Chapter 9

Paralyzed

It was not long before the power angels of the Lord acted quickly, subdued all flight and military bases in and around where Jesus and the riders were! The angels, as well as some of the horses and riders, flew quickly into and above the bases with powerful light knocking out all the electronics of the jets and aviation.

They were paralyzed with the light so that no military personnel could even get to their jets. Everything was at a standstill.

A couple of jets flew across the Mediterranean Sea from another country. The angels quickly subdued them.

Jesus, with his winged horses, flew above the lands. Then Jesus sent a shout and bolt of light mightily upwards that the archangels, around in the skies of the earth saw this, with this bolt and shout of mighty light, they started at speeds of light to encircle the earth like Jericho, with tremendous power upon the waters and lands of the earth.

Riders on winged horses with angels flew and continued to fly to military bases, airports around the earth. Earth had already experienced many battles, but as these riders came, the soldiers knew that the day of the Lord had come. The riders flashed great bolts of light to warn the bases of their presence. Mighty angels released powerful bolts of light towards the base. Winds and destruction was high in the area before they even arrived, so resistance was low! The riders opened up with mighty bolts of light towards the soldiers that attempted to fight.

They sought out any ships and quickly bolted light unto the carriers destroying the planes. Many soldiers laid and prayed that the destruction would stop. They knew they could not fight this mighty power.

Thousands of angels and power riders were in the skies at these bases.

The archangels and other power angels continued to encircle the earth at speeds of light.

The ears and mouths of personnel in all military bases were made so they could not hear or speak. The armies that were in the fields of battle at or about Israel were rendered deaf and dumb. They could not hear, neither could they speak a word. Only moan and groan as these were the only sounds! Many of the people all over the earth experienced the same thing. They were trying to speak with all their might, but they could not!

Wee Angel said, "My! What has the Lord done so quickly!"

Then Jesus, with a great light and booming voice, sent a flash of light outward, and the winged riders flew closer to the lands of the earth as the people started to see horses and riders in the skies. Flashes of light, lightning appeared to people all over the earth. Other riders proceeded closer to areas where separation by angels had already been done. Angels had come to earth in this season, to separate the tares and as written in the Word.

Now, as the riders came, they swooped close to the treetops, being seen by certain ones that had gone against and lead many to destroy his ways. The horses would fly, and they would entwine the person or group, so they could not move. The riders brought them to death if there was resistance or fired upon by anyone. They flew through the streets, cornering those on the run! They continued to destroy any opposition as necessary!

The leaders continued to send angels with power to military bases. Also, riders on the winged horses circled the bases subduing any resistance with light that bolted like lightning from their heavenly power. As commanded, they spoke words known to mankind and light bolted from them towards the aircraft and soldiers that gathered to fight. The soldiers learned very quickly the strength of the power they were trying to fight! Around the earth, everything was being brought to a standstill!

These angels of power worked together with the riders on the winged horses. The soldiers could see some of the angels, but most could not see the mighty angels in flight or on the ground. The riders were more visible to man with the tremendous power of the light that shone all around them. The Lord wanted mankind to see these riders and horses.

The archangels continued to circle the earth at speeds of light with a tremendous noise. This was like the thunder of heaven ripping through trees and homes with pieces flying everywhere. Everyone was feeling the power of the archangels. Many were crawling around, trembling in fear.

The earth as Jericho was being brought to its knees very quickly! Many all over the earth were on their knees praying for mercy.

Matthew and Obadiah flew their horses with the angels by their sides across some of the lands by Israel. They saw military men and women on their knees in prayer, guns laid by their sides. They were in prayer, now hoping for God's mercy as Jesus had finally come to bring justice to all mankind.

Daniel Leske

Chapter 10

Jesus Carries Out God's Will

They flew to many areas and saw people that seemed to be blinded, but others were not. Those who were not blinded seemed perfectly fine and were praying because they knew THE DAY OF THE LORD HAD COME!

As this happened, Jesus had certain angels bringing those that endured everything that had happened into church basement shelters for protection.

There were days of darkness on earth with the dragon in his anger raging about the cities on earth. He stirred up the winds of hate. He also stirred up the winds of the earth with his tail of power, creating tornadoes of blackness that filled the skies. He swooped amongst these storms of darkness. He flew with other dragon-like creatures over and through the cities. Blood flew across the buildings as the storm destroyed them as well as many people.

Blood! Blood! Blood!~

Even those in shelters were not safe as the demonic powers found many to terrorize and destroy!

The tares were not protected like the wheat.

Around the earth, small and large groupings of the Lord's people were hiding and living as best they could while a seemingly evil destruction of forces and armies on earth were against them. They had separated like the wheat and were being protected by angels that were close to their camps.

Lucifer knew this and was out to destroy them as best he could with his fallen angels.

He had many deceived and finding ways to entrap them as well as destroy them. He had pushed the governments and military into this position.

In these days, when the dragon felt Jesus was coming with his army, he went to the cities and lands to destroy many that helped him in ways that are not pleasing to mankind.

In his rage, more houses, areas of cities were under attack by the dragon. He drew his tail, carried more serpents, alligators, snakes, reptiles and flung them into populated areas.

He raged with mankind slaying others, becoming massive and common as the enemy knew his time was short on earth.

He flew about, over and above, saying, "Mine! Mine! Mine! You are all mine! My souls! My kingdom!"

The dragon went after ships, trains, airplanes, cars, schools, cities, towns, with massive slayings to appease his anger and rage. Blood seemed to flow by the killings!

These angels had already been sent to earth with the Archangels were separating away from his people. The angels brought many to the cities along with Israel to be protected by other guardian angels.

He had them already into deep prayer on earth, because they knew something was coming to them, and that Jesus was coming with his army.

They were prepared in their hearts as they stayed in prayer, waiting for the Lord to return to earth. As in his homeland, and this was all the countries. God separated those of his own that made it through the times till his return to earth.

Now the battle was real! Jesus was back at earth!

As the Archangels continued with great power, going around the earth. Dust was in the air filling the skies till the sun was very red and very black in some areas as it flew upwards, the waters of the ocean at this time are in a roar as never before seen by man.

The archangels kept up the noise from their wings. With this, Jesus had his winged horses and riders fly more on the lands. They flew lower above the lands. He was in front, riding on his horse named Revelation. He flew to where the armies had been in battle. He flew very slowly, coming up over the horizon to them.

As he flew, those of the armies saw him as a great warrior that has come to earth. Those of his people, as they looked up to see him on the white horse, they saw him with blood streaming down his face and body.

They saw that it looked like thorns on his head. They saw his clothes spotted with blood and his flesh ripped by what he had gone through for them. These people of this army and others knew then that the one on the donkey was now back, but the one on the white horse was the SON OF GOD.

All others as they saw Jesus on Revelation with formation of winged horses across and along the horizon, saw the warrior Jesus Christ, the King of Kings. They were all on their knees whether they were in the armies or not.

Jesus was on earth and close to it yet he was not going to land Revelation until everything was done.

With this Jesus, Wee Angel, Felicia, Angel Gabriella, and Angel Daniella on their winged horses slowly flew higher again away from this area of his homeland.

"My! Oh, My!" Felicia kept saying, "My! Oh my! We just saw Jesus return to his people and the start of something great!"

Tears flowed from her eyes as all of them were awed by Jesus. THEY KNEW HE HAD TO RETURN STRONG TO EARTH BECAUSE OF SO MANY NOT BELIEVING IN HIM.

The tears flowed as much was yet to happen around them. Each one knew this as Wee Angel talked to Matthew, and each one spoke to the one they were riding with about this mission.

They quietly tried to smile as best they could in all this.

The skies were dark, but the sun was full. Darkened by the dusts and power of the archangels as they still swept around the earth, keeping all mankind in its place so that the winged horses and riders with angels could finish their mission.

Daniel Leske

Chapter 11

After the Dragon

With this, Matthew, Obadiah knew now that Jesus would be going after the dragon of the earth as well as others he would use to fight in his army against the Lord's army. The dusts of the earth were still stirring mightily around the earth as Jesus, and the riders became more ready to finish their mission.

Jesus, with the winged horses and riders, slowly flew upwards away from his homeland to a land far away.

Jesus knew that Lucifer would not be waiting where he would enter earth for Lucifer knew he was coming because of all the turbulence that the archangels had already done around and with the winds of the earth.

Jesus, with the formation of winged horses and riders flew onward higher and higher above the waters of the Mediterranean Sea, and with time they flew above the waters of the mighty Atlantic Ocean. Angels to their sides followed this mighty formation of white-winged horses.

David and Joshua, with their formations of horses, onward the massive formation flew towards a mighty land on earth that Jesus had given the power and the people to do his mighty will on earth, the United States of America.

Now, the land had backslidden to the point that Judgment had come to his own land. They had fallen away from his divine will in many ways, and they had become more like the Babylon of the earth rather than the glories of God Almighty.

The people had fought and fought to keep Christ as the front of their country, but power by Lucifer had gained control of many parts of this mighty nation. Jesus had formed it to be a nation under his power as the son of God.

Jesus knew this as he flew along over the ocean. The riders knew this, and they were on a mission to free this, his homeland, as Israel, yet now they were going to release the bondage of this his land he started and made great under his name.

Onward they flew! They saw ahead in the high skies blackness by the power of the enemy. They saw flames of blackness high into the skies of this land.

The skies had billowing smoke flying and rising upwards.

As the riders approached Lucifer's army, they could see the whirlwinds of little dragon-like creatures, snake-like bats, and serpents flying in the clouds of blackness that had already stirred the lands around the earth.

Before the arrival of the Lord's army, archangels had already been to earth. Lucifer had taken many of earth's people with him by his ways of deception. Earth was in turmoil because of Lucifer's power to deceive and destroy! His destruction was significant to the wellbeing of the earth. It was because of this the elders with Jesus made a decision about the earth and the wellbeing of the elect that was on earth.

Fires and flames from the dragon and his army had already caused heavy damage in this place because of what was about to happen! Jesus had formations of white-winged horses come to the west shores of this mighty nation. As these formations that Jesus was leading drew close, they saw a huge bomb explode high in the sky. Then the dragon with a huge body and slithering like serpents flew all about him.

Jesus knew Lucifer would be putting everything he had from Hell for this battle.

The slither, snake-like forms about his head like a crown of fire that were pitch black with red flames coming out through the black flames of fire.

They saw other serpent-like forms fly upward from the horizon with powerful forms of angelic like beings that had blackened faces and armor of coal-black body shields. There were black flames that swirled about them as they rode beasts of the reptilian world.

Small dragon-like creatures that walked and slithered yet could still fly at speeds of the spirit world. The dragon flew more upward and higher above Jesus with the winged horses that flew to the sides, and at the same time, stayed a distance from Lucifer and his formations, as more of these forms filled the skies. Black smoke! Black smoke, fires, red flames, filled the skies. Black clouds were high above!

Serpents in-flight crowded the skies away from Jesus, yet still over this mighty shores of this land.

Jesus and his winged horses were still over the waters of this mighty ocean.

Chapter 12

The Battle Continues

Archangel Michael and Archangel Raphael were close to the formations to protect Jesus if needed! Flames of black fire-like light flew at the formations, yet power deflected the flames aside. Laughter and cursing from Lucifer followed as he slowed, and roared.

To the west of this mighty country, other formations of white-winged horses and riders already were there.

Abraham was there with his group of riders.

The dragon saw the Lord's winged horses and riders approaching him.

Crowds of people stood and watched by towns and fields, looking at the skies.

The dragon soared at them with mighty speed, slaying them quickly with his fire, and power of his tail.

Bodies were in flight everywhere by his power. Trees burned and exploded quickly! Winds blew like a hurricane to the fields as people crawled for safety!

The sky was black, the sun so none could hardly see! Other fallen angels hurled black light of explosion to the grounds and fields. Damage everywhere as the fallen angels raged! More blood!

They hurled black rays of power into the skies towards the forces of angels and winged horses. Black bolts of tars and smoke flew past the horses. Some were shaken, while others lost flight and headed to the ground.

The riders flew onward in formation with bolts from Lucifer's army coming at them. More horses and riders lost flight and headed towards the ground. Many stunned but remained in flight!

The riders kept formation and flew onward!

The dragon, like an atomic bomb, exploded with power a high cloud of smoke that billowed upwards like a mushroom. The areas close on earth were receiving heavy damage from the tremendous explosions of power. Trees and houses, buildings, fields of dust, vehicles exploded and shredded by the awesome power there.

More horses and riders were shaken by the bolts from the fallen angels.

They flew onward, closer and closer to the dragon's army.

Then in a moment, Archangel Michael flew up to the riders quickly!

He sent several bolts of light, and then a mighty bolt of light at the dragon.

The dragon's head ripped side to side from the hit. The dragon was stunned for a short time but recovered. He knew then that Archangel Michael was there.

The dragon circled his army, letting them know that they would be in flight away from the area.

Archangel Michael flew towards Wee Angel, Felicia, Angel Daniella, and Angel Gabriella.

He flew close to them and nodded to them with a smile on his face. They knew he had waited a long time for this.

Other angels sent powerful bolts of light towards the fallen angels!

The army of Lucifer was slowly losing strength by the bolts coming from the angels of God. The riders as well sent powerful bolts of light at the fallen angels.

Fallen angels on serpents were hit and fell towards earth. When they hit the earth, they flew right into it, disappearing below the surface. More of Lucifer's army were hit by the riders on the horses. Their flight continued closer toward their enemies.

More from both sides went downward!

Angels were already there chasing down and after demons that were trying to flee the area. These horses and angels swooped close to the land, held and bound the demon with a light that quickly encircled the demons and bound them with heavenly swords of fire that these riders had beside them.

The fire of this light came out of the flaming sword, flew straight and quickly banded the devil or demon tightly and many banded together like the binding of wheat. These were the devils and Jesus had them bound so that order could be restored on earth.

An angel or two would stay and guard them until all was done. The people on earth could not see them bound, for they still were spirit so mankind could not see this.

The winged horses and riders came more across in mighty formations as the angels caught more and more demonic beings and serpents tied them, bound them, put them together like a bundle so they could be guarded there.

Lucifer knew this was occurring, so he shot more fire past Jesus and his riders.

The power of God was there at this mighty land. Demons that were in certain people came ripping out of their flesh, leaving the person staggering, and in some cases, very severely damaged as the flesh would cut or tear open from this. There was death to many as well!

Then Lucifer's army of thousands of blackened fallen angels with the dragon in the front flew northward out and away from this land.

It was like a black comet or smoke and power as they flew out across the ocean away from Jesus. Several of them tried to shoot their fires at the winged horses, but the flames were put out by the tremendous light of their shields.

Lucifer fired a tremendous ball of light, black light that caused the horses and riders to loose flight for a short time. They recovered and soon riders were in flight again!

The trail of serpent-like creatures had seemingly l000's of demon's attacked to their being like parasites as they flew onward!

Jesus and the riders at this time still watched, waited and watched them.

Lucifer, the black cloud of fallen angels, flew northward, headed towards Europe. Jesus, the riders, angels and archangels all followed at a distance.

Chapter 13

The Chase as the Battle Continues

Then in time, as Lucifer flew over Europe, damage was done everywhere. Trees were uprooted, buildings destroyed in their path. It seems he was going to damage as much as he could as the black comet-like cloud of fallen angels, demons, devils and everything else one could imagine flew over Europe, headed towards the Lord's homeland. Bodies were hanging in trees, with pools of blood everywhere!

Jesus, riders, angels, archangels, continued to follow at a distance as the dragon flew onward. Jesus had other winged horses and riders with angels and another archangel, so the dragon continued east around Israel and to the middle east countries located east of Israel.

Those that caused so much turmoil to his homeland. Here the dragon saw on the eastern horizon more riders winged horses, angels, and archangels. The time was getting where the dragon knew he was cornered and knew his time was short.

Angels had already stepped in with the power of God Almighty, in that they had made it so Lucifer couldn't go out and away from earth. As this happened, any and all devils, serpents, demons that were trying to escape were being subdued with tremendous light from the winged horses and riders and powerful angels.

They were being spiritually bound in this light from the flaming swords of the riders. The 1,000's of fallen angels were close by the dragon, and their blackness of withering in itself was horrifying to the eyes of everyone.

Again, small serpents flew in the airs, crawling lizards, with fallen angels on their backs. They fired black power fires everywhere at the horses, but the light subdued these blows by the dragon. This time, Jesus made sure that the devil's rays and fires from his mouth of many heads could not and would not stop his army.

The dragon and his army were now close to the area of Babylon, as so stated in the Bible. The dragon roared upward past Jesus and shouted, cursed at all the riders.

Archangel Michael hurled a beam of tremendous light at Lucifer as it seemed to stun Lucifer for a short timely

Then he hurled a mighty bolt of black light at Archangel Michael as it exploded close to him, and then he was stunned by this. Both knew their power was equal.

Dragon, who was angered by Archangel Michael, said, "Why didn't you join us?"

Then fires were all over everywhere as the fallen angels of the dragon unleashed tremendous black balls of fires that exploded close by the riders.

Some were thrown from their horses as the battle raged on. They spiraled downwards towards the earth in a ball of fire.

The battle rages, but Jesus only allowed this for a short time

He flew with Revelation towards the front and closer to the dragon and his army.

He then raised his right arm upwards. It was like heaven opened, and a great light power from the throne came flying downwards towards the army of the dragon. All were stunned by its mighty power.

Chapter 14

Evil Finally taken from Earth

The ground underneath them started to shake as if an earthquake was started and spread through the region quickly.

The grounds were now all flames from the fires below the earth as the armies of Jesus watched, and they circled the whole area. Many of the fallen angels flew and rode their beasts trying to escape, but were stopped by other angels, and the tremendous power of the riders on winged horses as they fired enormous bolts of light as they sat on the horses.

The bolts were like lightning, and the fallen angels were stunned mightily! Then more powerful light and fires from out of heaven came forth.

Jesus shouted, "Let it be done, Lucifer! You and your fallen angels, beast, and serpents will now be locked up for the next 1000 years, that we said we would do! So be it! Let it be done!"

Then more light appeared from the heavens. The skies were shaking and the ground was shaking!

All the riders and angels flew further back from the area from all the blasts by the dragon and God's mighty power. Then light from everywhere, fires of God Almighty and his right arm encircled the dragon and his army. The power of the son of God was all around, and then streams of light bound the dragon and bound the fallen angels, one at a time.

Then the ground lite with fires as it opened, cracked open, the dragon still cursing was now bound and all that were with him, including Jezebel. There were others on earth that had been bound by the angels, and all at once, those who were with Lucifer were lowered through the opening into the earth.

Then the archangels went and got a massive piece of rock from the mountains that God had ready just for this. It was like a mountain being moved. They lifted this gigantic rock and placed it over the opening just as the devil had done to Jesus at the cross.

They sealed the tomb of the devil and fallen angels.

Jesus said to a group of angels, "You stand guard at this seal, and we will guard this seal for 1000 years."

With this, Jesus said, "Let it be done!"

It seemed all of the earth heard this. Lord God Almighty made sure that evil could not come up to anyone through the ground. He made sure by his almighty power that the power of the enemy could not during the 1000 years come through the walls of the earth towards those remaining on the earth.

Daniel Leske

Chapter 15

Jesus at The Mount of Olives

All the angels were in jubilation as the enemy of mankind and heaven had been finally bound. Jesus was very quiet as Revelation flew towards David, Joshua, Solomon, Abraham, and leaders who flew slowly to Jesus. They nodded to Jesus. He quietly nodded as now the clouds of darkness gradually were replaced by the light of the day.

No matter what, Jesus' heart was heavy because with all of this had come destruction across the earth, and lives had been taken as well! In this season, much damage, warfare, bloodshed, storms, evil ways, evil killings, and all forms of evil that had been committed had forced him to make a decision. Then to carry it out meant more damage.

Jesus was very quiet.

Wee Angel, Felicia, Angel Gabriella, and Angel Daniella were so shocked in what they had seen, yet happy it was over because the work to restore earth was now beginning.

Jesus on Revelation flew quietly. Archangels Michael, Gabriel, Micah, and Raphael flew close to Jesus and said words of comfort to him.

He then led all the formations together as they slowly flew towards Jerusalem, as he promised in scripture. His heart was happy yet heavy, as they flew onward across the lands.

Then Jesus flew Revelation and said for the others to wait, as Revelation flew towards the Mount of Olives. Then slowly Revelation landed, and as Jesus got off him and his feet touched the Mount of Olives, a mighty bolt of lightning, wind, fire, and tremendous power from out of heaven split the mountain as slowly streams of water started to flow outward from its inside.

Jesus stood with Revelation watched as a smile came to the Lord's face.

Again, a loud earth moving noise resounded throughout Jerusalem as Jesus was finally here on earth to rule and restore it back to the Lord's ways.

Some of the walls of Jerusalem were shattered, as piles of rubble was all around it. Jerusalem would be restored as it was damaged through all that had taken place. But the Lord knew some of this would happen. He was going to rebuild anyway as he planned.

Slowly more riders on winged horses landed closer to Jerusalem.

Many went about with other angels to help restore and put in order a new life on earth. This would take time, but the angels and some of the riders were there ready to help.

Chapter 16

Jesus Quiet

Many horses with riders were somewhere close on these lands about Jerusalem. Most though were busy helping angels and helping every way possible to bring order around the earth.

Wee Angel, Felicia, Angel Gabriella, and Angel Daniella stood at a distance with Revelation, several angels, and other riders that had landed there.

Jesus, Joshua, David, Solomon, and the leaders of the horses talked on the Mount of Olives. It still was beautiful in every way as now some streams of water flowed through where it had been split and leveled. Olive trees and bushes began to blossom, and we could see that it would become a very plush garden.

Within heaven's time as Jesus was in a lot of conversation with these leaders, a man slowly walked through, between rocks, bushes, and lands with several others towards Jesus. As they neared Jesus, the others remained as this man with a beard walked closer to Jesus.

Jesus knew him, and right away, a big smile came across Jesus' face . The two hugged a heavenly hug as they greeted each other, for the moment was very special.

Both Wee Angel and Felicia looked at this man and wondered with great wonder! They knew something about him, yet they could not speak about it. Then from out amongst the other women and a couple of men came two little girls. They came up beside Jesus and this man.

Angel Daniella and Angel Gabriella saw they were twin girls just about their size.

"Look, Felicia," said Wee Angel, "They're twins and identical twins."

Then the two girls, after hugs with Jesus, came towards Angel Daniella and Angel Gabriella.

"What're your names?" asked Angel Daniella.

One said, "I'm Daniella!"

The other said, "I'm Gabriella!"

"So are we!" both angel girls said.

Then many hugs, laughter, and much joy filled their hearts with Wee Angel and Felicia joined in too with them. Then in time, this man with the beard walked closer to Wee Angel and Felicia. They looked at him. He looked and greeted them. Then smiled, nodded to them. They nodded, ran, and greeted him with more hugs.

Then with time, he, the two twin girls, and the others slowly walked away towards Jerusalem and watched the scene of everyone by some olive trees.

All of them, together said, "Jesus, we love you so much!"

"Wee Angel and Angel Daniella flew to nearby bushes with some flowers. Picked them and gave them to Jesus. He had some tears in his eyes. His heart was joyful yet heavy!

Jesus said, "Thank you! I will see you again! I must go!"

They turned, waited, and watched everything.

They had tears in their eyes too!

The scene was special since Jesus had returned to earth his homeland.

Chapter 17

Doorway over Jerusalem

As they stood, with time, they saw in the distance coming from the west, clouds with tremendous light which came through the clouds. The clouds billowed high away from earth with feathery high and away towards heaven. The day had been long with so much as now it was closer to evening, and the skies with this opening to heaven had moved closer to Jerusalem and over Jerusalem.

It was the same opening that they saw the power of God capture Lucifer and his army. It now had moved over the lands of earth and as they watched, it was above Jerusalem. The light was so bright, that even though it was evening, it looked like daytime there at Jerusalem.

A new day, the darkness of this city was gone. The opening into heaven now had streams of light pouring towards Jerusalem.

Wee Angel said, "Look all of you."

Up at the sides of the clouds, they already saw glimpses of waterfalls of heaven, water, and steps of water, then it went away, just glimpses to their eyes of what was to happen there. Angels flew out through this doorway into the light. Some had carrying bags around their shoulders. They flew downward and above Jesus, and everyone else and were sprinkling seeds in flight.

Angel Gabriella said, "They're planting heavenly vegetation here. Thank you, Jesus!"

"Thank you, Jesus!" they all shouted!

They flew right over them, past them, around them, sprinkling seeds of heaven on the Mount of Olives.

Jesus turned to them and smiled.

The light was above Jerusalem with angels coming and going, more and more out of the huge opening of heaven that was now by earth and over Jerusalem and the Mount of Olives.

Angels sang glories to the Father, played instruments of praise.

The area was slowly becoming, and with time would be beautiful there as well as the glory of God.

They felt a fine mist of water from the clouds, as they had seen waterfalls, steps of water amongst the clouds. Every now and then a mist would fall over them — the beautiful heavenly mists of His waters.

"Look up!" said Felicia. "They look like gems in the clouds of light."

"Yes!" the others agreed.

The gem-like crystals were high amongst the clouds, gems from heaven that they knew would be a part of this new Jerusalem for the millennium, as Jesus was now on earth again! There were blues, greens, reds, aqua colors of light from these gems in the clouds above, that circled the light as it glowed over and around this city.

Holiness was felt everywhere now that the enemy of earth and mankind had been captured and taken away from all life on earth.

Chapter 18

A New Day for Earth

Within time, after many good days, they were ready to head back to heaven. Jesus had told David to take Revelation as he thought he would like to be with Wee Angel and Felicia.

Soon David with Felicia on Revelation were in the sky just above the Mount of Olives. All of them were soon in the skies, with many white-winged horses behind them.

Many riders stayed with Jesus and the others too!

They flew upwards into the light above the city, and soon they were in flight through the doorway and into the beautiful light stream headed back to God's Holy City. The mission was done and they were in flight in this light.

Onward in this light!

David and Joshua with their little passengers flew onward.

Soon in heaven's time, they came to heaven's lands where the beautiful Holy City was, and after time they landed outside the city on some grass, close to another gate to God's City. The feeling to be back close to the city was awesome for all of them.

David and Joshua were to seek out Paul and the elders to let them know about everything. They gave hugs to Wee Angel, Felicia, Angel Gabriella and Angel Daniella, then headed into the city. All were joyous and very happy to be back on heaven's lands.

David said, "We will see you again!"

He and Joshua smiled at them. They stayed with Revelation for a time, and then in heaven's time, the four headed into God's City to a special service being held in celebration. They went through the doorways into this service.

They saw celestial glories along the sides of God's Mountain. They saw thousands and thousands of angels gathered along the sides of God's Mountain. This sanctuary was in God's Holy City between bluffs of his mountain where the most beautiful golden lights glowed behind all the angels that were along and up the sides of this mighty valley around his mountain.

Saints were in praise with instruments of glory to the Father with praises by everyone there.

All four of them were so awed by this. Tears were in their eyes. Their hearts had gone through so much, yet this was the mighty comfort to them because of these special angels, the saints in praise, and the glory of God.

The angels, the heavenly glories, hallelujahs to the king, hallelujah's to God Almighty!

Hallelujahs they sang! The victory was finally theirs.

"Hallelujah to Jesus!" "Thank you, Jesus!" They sang as the angels played instruments with the sounds of trumpets, all along the miles and miles of this valley with thousands and thousands of angels in praise to the Father.

In heaven's time, Wee Angel and the others were close to a vast platform with the elders there. Joshua and David were with these elders, and soon Paul came out to speak, and the angels all became quiet in one accord as this happened throughout the valley.

Paul looked at Wee Angel and the others, then the elders.

He said, "The time has come that earth and heaven almost be one. It is a time for restoration, and much has to be done there. The victory is ours! Many have fought for this time to be! The glory of Christ, the glory of Jesus, has finally come to earth. Thank you, angels, saints, little ones, elders for everything that you have done to help glorify the kingdom of heaven. God bless!"

With this, he hugged our little ones that were waiting by the elders. Then the glories. Singing again rang loud by all the angels and saints.

David and Joshua said to Wee Angel, Felicia, Angel Gabriella, and Angel Daniella, "Go, there are some friends for you outside of the Gate with many Roses just for you."

Chapter 19

Wee Angel, Felicia, Angel Daniella and Angel Gabriella back to Friends

Angel Daniella, Angel Gabriella, Felicia, and Wee Angel were outside on a golden road that went away from God's Holy City.

There was a stream that wound amongst beautiful rose arbors on both sides of this road — twin waterfalls on each side that went upwards into part of God's Holy Mountain. Beautiful fruit trees lined both sides of the road. Glories filled the skies above them. Doves flew past them.

Several other saints passed by them, greeting them with good-days.

Angels flew over them on their way to more of this heavenly celebration of God's beauty and yet now a triumph in that earth would become beautiful in ways it had never known since its creation.

"All of us have been through a lot!" said Wee Angel.

The others nodded quietly.

They took time to pray, as Angel Gabriella prayed, "Father, help us now to be strong as we go about here in heaven. We pray for those on earth, and Jesus, and all that are helping him."

Each looked at each other, smiled, some tears flowed down their cheeks. The quietness of the moment.

Many roses, hedges, were along the waterfalls. Roses everywhere! There was some beautiful apple, orange trees, and also some grapes close to them.

Everything plush and rich in God's mighty heaven. Their hearts were so full! The tears kept flowing, as they knew that everything was good, and they were so thankful!

All of them in time as they started to realize the strength of their friendship, Wee Angel said, "Felicia, you and I have seen so much around heaven. Angel Gabriella and Angel Daniella have been with us several times. We have prayed together, had fellowship together. We have gone with the Lord together. It started when you came into that field of lilies."

Felicia said, "I know that! Oh my! Oh my! I said that so much as I have enjoyed so much here in heaven. The beauty is awesome here. Look at everything around us. It explains how beautiful our home is here."

All of them walked along the way for a while, looking at everything around them, seeing God's lands of creation. The beautiful grass, the fragrance of the flowers, winged horses, and riders in flight. Other horses were in the distance.

The glories of heaven were always there!

They walked on!

They kept up their talking, reflecting on everything that they have been a part of as they traveled together as friends.

Soon in heaven's time, an angel flew towards them. It was Angel Heather. She gave them hugs and flew onward, then Angel Rebecca flew up to them and flew onward. Then Angel Michelle, Angel Angelina, Angel Hannah, and Angel Jennifer flew up to them and flew onward to God's City.

Each one said to them that they had some special friends waiting on a beautiful courtyard that had waterfalls, plush grass, hedges of roses, beautiful hills, and bluffs in the distance with waterfalls cascading to the lands.

They soon came to a golden path that led there, and so they walked more quickly for in this open area were many friends. They saw Revelation(Sir William) standing there waiting for them. They quickly flew to their friends: Tuddley Teddy, Annie, Toby, Sir William, Starbright, Golden, Majestic, Noah, Longstreet, Zach, Barnabus, Sir Mark, Berry, April and Hope

So many all stood for them. All of them flew around their little friends. Tears were in their eyes.

"I've got to stop crying so much!" said Felicia.

The other three agreed.

"We have been crying a lot," answered Wee Angel.

Felicia gave Tuddley a big hug! Wee Angel gave Annie a big hug! Angel Daniella gave Sir William a big hug! Golden got a big hug! The little bears flew around all of them. They continued to hug and play with each one. The animals came up to them and put their heads by them.

Even they seemed to have a tear of joy in their eyes. Oh, they were so happy to see Wee Angel and Felicia again. They were so happy they smiled as animals would smile in their own ways. Glories streamed God's Holy City. This love and joy of God's heaven.

Chapter 20

A Beautiful Ending as Heaven goes On

They stood, praised God, and praised the Lord for their friends. Soon a few smaller angels, just a little bigger than Wee Angel, landed and greeted them.

"I'm Angel Sherri!"

"I'm Angel Penny!"

"I'm Angel Ernie!"

"I'm Angel Clover!"

"I'm Angel Rose!"

"I'm Angel Ben!"

"We love you so much," they exclaimed!

Then they flew around the little ones sitting on Noah and Sir William. They sat and continued to talk! Then more little angels flew up to them.

Wee Angel, with a big smile, said, "Where are they coming from?"

Felicia wondered too!

Then some more little angels flew up to them from along the golden path — all of them just a little bigger than Wee Angel.

More flew up to them.

"I'm Angel Jordan!"

"I'm Angel Stacy!"

"I'm Angel Bell!"

Each took a moment to greet Wee Angel and Felicia, as well as Angel Daniella and Angel Gabriella.

Hugs were given to them. Tears flowed, for the joy of heaven again was so strong in their hearts. There were little angels sitting by trees, sitting on Noah, Longstreet, Toby, Sir William, and Tuddley. They were sitting on everyone that they could sit on!

They flew around, up and over everything. More little angels flew into the area from above the trees.

"I'm Angel Twinkle!"

"I'm Angel Trinity!"

"I'm Angel Light!"

as they flew and hovered close by everyone.

"Thank you, Wee Angel!"

"Thank you, Felicia!"

"Thank you, Angel Daniella!"

"Thank you Angel Gabriella!"

Each one would say to them.

"Thank you, Revelation!"

"Thank you, Toby!"

"Thank you, Annie!"

"Thank you, Tuddley!"

More little angels flew into the area, more angels and more angels as all just a little bigger than Wee Angel.

More little angels!

They were everywhere!

"I'm Angel Bennie"

"I'm Angel Angeline!"

"I'm Angel Davy!"

"I'm Angel Kattie!"

"I'm Angel Melody!"

"I'm Angel Proverbs!"

"I'm Angel Maria!"

"I'm Angel Josh!"

"Thank you, Felicia!"

"Thank you, Wee Angel!"

"Thank you Angel Gabriella and Angel Daniella!"

"Thank you! Thank you! Thank you! Thank you!"

Some of them had roses in their hands. They were putting them in all the animals and Majestic too!

They gave some to Felicia, Wee Angel, Angel Daniella and Angel Gabriella.

"Thank you! Thank you! Thank you"

Oh, they flew around and around! Oh, the joy of heaven was ringing with love!

The glories above were mighty from the Lord's City.

More little angels flew singing glories to the Father as some played instruments.

The glories of God were strong there.

"Thank you, Wee Angel!"

"Thank you, Felicia!"

"Thank you!"

The joy of heaven was there. The moment was special. Tuddley Teddy, Noah, Revelation, Annie ...... again came close to them.

Each wiggled with all their might, their love and appreciation to them. Doves flew by them.

Felicia said, "Wee Angel, the love and joy of heaven is here."

They were giggling, laughing, crying!

"We have so much to be thankful for here," said Wee Angel as the others agreed.

Soon all the little angels started to fly away from them.

"Thank you, Wee Angel!"

"Thank you, Felicia!"

"Thank you! Thank you," the little angels kept saying as they flew on!

Soon it was just the little friends with Wee Angel, Felicia, Angel Daniella, and Angel Gabriella.

Their hearts were full. They prayed together, they smiled together, and they praised the Lord together.

They played with the animals. So much joy and love in their little hearts.

Glories of God above them. The waters continued to flow past them.

"We have been having a wonderful time," said Wee Angel.

"I know that!" so softly whispered Felicia.

Angel Daniella and Angel Gabriella agreed as they stood in a circle with tears, holding hands, with all the little friends close by them.

All of them enjoyed and were a part of this MIGHTY JOY OF HEAVEN.

GOD BLESS EVERYONE OF YOU THAT READ THIS! LIFE ON EARTH WILL NOT BE QUITE THE SAME AFTER THIS, BUT HEAVEN IS THERE FOR YOU AND FRIENDS LIKE THESE.

From the Author

The Joy of Heaven 7 is written so there may be a little time before this happens, yet as the writer I feel this time may not be long, as more happens and has happened on earth.

The Lord can tarry in carrying this out, depending strictly on his grace and the promises to the time as stated in the Bible. Still this is only a matter of years, and not a very long time in comparison to life on earth since the beginning of life.

The Lord will come and when he does, he will be as he so spoke, and this day that had been talked about by the prophets

We have the Word of God and so we cannot deny the intensity of this when it occurs and he told us.

IN THESE TIMES stay close to the Trinity as defined by the Word.

DANIEL

www.ingramcontent.com/pod-product-compliance
Lightning Source LLC
LaVergne TN
LVHW081326060426

835511LV00011B/1876